RENEW, REFOCUS AND RECOVER!

A ROAD TRIP TO THE LIFE YOU DESERVE

BY
RAQUEL R. ROBINSON

Dedication

With a heart full of
memories and gratitude,
I dedicate this book to my Dad

**Willie R. McFerson
(Mac)**

(1945-1998)

CONTENTS

Section Three: Recovering

Section Four:Ready

ACKNOWLEDGEMENTS

Writing this book has been a part of my own road trip. I am so grateful that I did not have to take this journey alone. God has blessed me from birth with absolutely wonderful mentors, role models, and friends. He continues to bring people into my life that encourage me to be who I am and to live the life that I am called to live. I'd like to take this opportunity to thank my Success Team for this project:

- My husband, Henry L. Robinson. Your love and support these past ten years has made all of the difference in my life. You are my reminder that God does hear and answer my prayers, and then some.

- My parents, Willie and Lillie McFerson. Mom, thank you and Dad for the awesome example of partnership and love. We miss Dad a lot, but he would be so proud of us. Thanks for your prayers and encouragement during this project.

- My copy editor, Dr. Carolyn Hull Anderson. Dr. Anderson, thank you for adding yet another thing to your heaping plate and agreeing to copy edit this work. My thanks is no Mercedes Benz, but my gratitude holds the same value in my heart.

- Russell (Rashaad) McFerson. You are so much more than my little brother. You are a man full of wisdom and amazing talent and insight. Thank you for your love and wisdom on this journey.

- Rev. Queen Esther Thomas. I have learned so much from you about God and myself. Thank you for your generosity and for nurturing my gifts.

- Many thanks to my newest friend, Aimee Laramore. You are right - iron does sharpen iron. Thanks for rubbing against me.

- Barbara McGee. Thank you for being there. Knowing that you are only a ten minute drive away is a great blessing.

- My coaches, Valorie Burton and W. Rollin Henderson, Jr. Valorie, you helped bring clarity about other situations so that my womb was clear, finally, to give birth to this project. Rollin, thank you so much for your counsel and ear. Your kindness, wisdom, and genuineness will never be forgotten.

- Pam Perry. Thank you for sharing your marketing and public relations expertise to keep me on the right track.

- To my number one fans, Alexandria (7) and Michael (3). You two make me believe that I can do anything. Thanks for sharing my time and attention so that I could complete this project. And yes, Lexi, if I need pictures for my next book, you can be the illustrator.

Most of all, I thank God for being patient with me on my quest and journey to purpose. Thank you for allowing me to be the lamp through which Your light shines.

INTRODUCTION

I started writing this book about nine years ago. The original title was Journey Out of the Zone: Lighting the Way to Your Destiny. I started writing the book after doing what I then thought was moving out of my comfort zone. I had just moved away from home for the very first time. I had managed to earn both a bachelor's and master's degree without leaving the comfort of my parents' home. So being married and moving to a small rural town in upstate New York seemed like a real journey out of my comfort zone.

Nine years later, I realize that I have learned a tremendous amount since then. I have learned that there is no such thing as a comfort zone. I have learned my true purpose and passion. And I most certainly have developed the ability to discern the difference between my timing and God's timing. It wasn't until I began to reach the end of this project that I discovered there is no such thing as a comfort zone.

I was having a conversation with my financial coach, W. Rollin Henderson, Jr., about my philosophy regarding the comfort zone. The comfort zone serves as a cocoon when used as a time of preparation, but it becomes a coffin if you never emerge and become the butterfly that you were created to be. I was so pleased with how poetic that sounds. Then

Rollin said, "Raquel, do you really believe that? There is no such thing as a comfort zone. The myth of the comfort zone is the coffin." He meant that living beneath your ability and purpose is never comfortable. There will always be a longing and tugging to explore the possibilities that exist. The possibilities and our potential are endless. But we make the choice to remain in what I now call the *discomfort zone.*

If any man be in Christ, he is a new creature: old things are passed away and; behold things have become new (2 Corinthians 5:17). There is no cocooning process with God. When you accept Him into your heart, you automatically become a butterfly. This revelation was helpful to me personally and will keep me from perpetuating this myth and lie in my service to others.

An exciting aspect of this road trip has been the discovery of my purpose. I have a diverse cross section of skills, education, and gifts. Sometimes, it is challenging to see how they all fit together. Through, patience, prayer, and study, God has been just as anxious to reveal it to me as I have been to discover it. God has called me to be a lamp that holds the very glory and light of God. Like John the Baptist, I am only the lamp, and Jesus is the light (John 1: 8 KJV, John 5:35 AMP). So I hold the glory of God in the path of the people that I serve. The source of the light is the very presence of the spirit of God that lives within them.

Even after discovering my purpose, it took some time to discern the method of delivery and timing to move forward. I know that I am to serve others through speaking, writing, and personal coaching. The speaking and writing were more in line with my education and professional background. My husband introduced me to the coaching profession. While completing my training as a professional life coach, I could see very quickly how developing my gift of encouragement will strengthen my ability to live my purpose. All of these things prompted my husband and me to start our coaching practice, Making a Change LLC. I find it an honor and privilege to hold a lamp of encouragement over the path of my clients so they can identify clearly their next steps - for themselves.

Finally, I have learned that my timing and God's timing are very different. My timing is derived, and His timing is divine. After nine years of sporadic writing, I finished writing and compiling this manuscript in two weeks. There was a strong sense of urgency and responsibility to complete this project. This was not the ideal turnaround time for a project like this. But it was like a train that couldn't be stopped. No one on my Success Team would allow me to quit. May you be blessed by my obedience.

This book is written to anyone who feels the same urgency to move forward in God's purpose that I felt to complete this project. There is a burning desire in you, to move from your discomfort zone and renew, refocus and recover. I am writing to individuals who want to live their purpose *on* purpose. I am writing to people who want to live the life they deserve - today. My goal is to prepare you for the journey that God will use to lead you to manifest His promise to you. This is not a step by step guide for how to grow your business or find a mate. It's an exploration of who you are, what you value, and how to be true to that.

Each chapter is a combination of my own experiences and transparencies, some personal coaching, and an opportunity for your own personal reflection. I encourage you to pause for reflection before moving on to the next chapter. Because I am merely the lamp and Jesus is the true light, I have included a lamp for your feet in each chapter, something for you to ponder. But most importantly, I have included scripture to serve as the light for your pathway.

I want this book to be a reminder of how wonderful God created you to be. You are perfectly equipped right now. You simply need someone to hold the light for you. Thank you for that privilege. I am not certain if you are just starting your road trip or if you are stranded on the side of the road. But my prayer is that by the time you complete this book, God's glory will be incredibly bright in your life. As a result, you will take your next steps with certainty and boldness. Are you ready? I'll light the way.

SECTION ONE
RENEWING

T o renew means to make like new, to restore to freshness, vigor, or perfection (Merriam- Webster Online
Dictionary 2005-2006). If you were preparing for a vacation,
you would never consider taking dirty and outdated clothing.
The same is true for us on our road trip to the life we deserve.
In this section, we will focus on returning to the newness of
our commitment and restoring our mind.

CHAPTER ONE
MAKE THE DECISION
TO TRAVEL

The preparation for our road trip begins with making the decision to travel. This decision requires you to make the conscious choice to move out of your discomfort zone and commit to making a change. You will recall that I discussed the myth and lie of the comfort zone. When we remain stagnant and paralyzed by fear, we are never comfortable. We are in a state of discomfort or a discomfort zone. We spend most of our lives in this discomfort zone because we have developed a tolerance for the discomfort of fear and apathy. We choose this discomfort over the discomfort of exploring the pathway to the life we want.

Because you are reading these pages, I know that you have a desire to travel. So let's move that desire to a renewed commitment to start anew with vigor. How you come to that commitment will be based on your own experiences and circumstances. I made this decision for myself after penning these thoughts:

"My Personal Decision"

The fruit of the Spirit is love, joy, peace, patience, kindness, goodness, faithfulness, gentleness, and self-control (Galatians 5:22-23 NIV). When I think of the fruit of the Spirit, I envision a wonderful bowl of fruit, perfect in color and size. It is perfect and without harsh chemicals and pesticides- not tart and hard, but perfectly ripe. Even upon approach, you can smell the fresh aroma of the sweet fruit. You can identify the smell of each fruit.

When I think about the fruit basket on my kitchen table, there is very little variety. I don't eat fruit regularly, so I keep some fruit in the refrigerator to preserve it longer. The others that are kept in the basket look pretty good for about a week. Then they begin to darken and lose their form because they weren't consumed at their peak. As for the fruit in the refrigerator, it is often forgotten to rot in the produce drawer.

Another disturbing aspect of the fruit basket on the kitchen table is that it often becomes a dish for non-fruit items. There are items such as ink pens, loose change, and business cards. The more rotten the fruit becomes, the more cluttered the basket becomes with these foreign objects. So I perpetuate the cycle again. I vow to eat more healthy foods. I buy lots of fruit from the market and promise to eat all of it. But by week's end, I am cleaning out a refrigerator full of discolored and disfigured nectarines, grapes, cherries, strawberries, and pineapple. And the basket on the kitchen table is full of rotten apples, overripe bananas, and other junk. I ask myself, "Why do you keep going through this?" Yes, fruit is a very impor-tant part of a healthy diet, but I never eat all that

I buy. I buy so much because I hate to run to the market every other day. So I buy what appears to be two weeks of fruit that I can not eat before it spoils.

On this particular day, as I tossed out the last of the rotten fruit, I thought about my spiritual fruit. I often treat it like my natural fruit. There are some that I bare regularly, and as you approach me, you can smell the sweet fragrance of the Spirit in my character. But there are others that remind me of the bruised fruit on the kitchen table. One in particular is faithfulness. I make a commitment to be faithful in the areas of my life where I constantly struggle. They include getting up faithfully at 5:30 A.M. for prayer, devotion, study, and meditation, and maintaining a healthy diet and exercise regimen. Rounding out the list is keeping the house tidy and clean and being delivered from procrastination.

So I start out with a bang. I buy new pens and highlighters for studying. I get new work out clothes, and I develop a new housekeeping schedule (I am the Queen of planning!). After about two weeks, 5:30 becomes 6:00 A.M. I have slipped on my exercise routine. The date-completed section of my house-keeping schedule is blank - I can't even find all of those highlighters that I bought! And I vow to start over next week (not today though!). And that would describe the fruit in my basket, so to speak. The others that I hoard in the refrigerator of my Spirit are peace and joy - tucked away and often forgotten. Who has peace and joy when faithfulness and self-control are rotting in a bowl (out in the open no less for everyone to see)?

That day I had had enough. I asked God to show me what to do. "Just buy enough fruit for today!" I seemed to hear the Spirit say. What a novel thought!

Buy only what you can consume in one day. It isn't a huge inconvenience to go to the store each day. The produce is in the front of the store. It is easily accessible. Besides, regular visits will ensure that I have access to the freshest fruit the grocer has to offer. Furthermore, Jesus taught us to pray, *give us this day, our daily bread (Matthew 6:11)*. He didn't tell us to ask for leftovers from yesterday's provision or a two-week supply so that we don't have to ask again for a while.

My prayer became, *Lord, give me enough fruit for today. Particularly, teach me to be faithful, one minute, one hour, and one day at a time. Teach me to be faithful with my time with you, my body, and taking care of my family, which includes housekeeping. Give me a TODAY versus tomorrow faithfulness - just enough fruit for today! Prevent my fruit from becoming soft and mushy. Keep my basket (my mind) from becoming cluttered with things that don't belong there. Deliver joy and peace from my spiritual refrigerator and display them in my basket with your other beautiful ripe fruit. When people approach me, allow them to smell each fruit individually. Most importantly, Lord, forgive me for the lack of faith that has accelerated the decay of other fruit in my life. I know that you forgive me, but it is so difficult to forgive myself for sleeping late, eating an entire carton of ice cream, and stacking one more glass in an already overflowing kitchen sink. Give me enough fruit for today to remove the guilt of yesterday's failures, and encourage me to press on one more minute, one more hour, one more day in the fruit of faithfulness. I will come to you daily to ensure that I have the freshest fruit that you have to offer. Thank you that I am a vessel of honor, suitable to house your provision of enough fruit for today!*

This was my first published article. I submitted it to a fellow writer for review, and she published it in her weekly column in a local newspaper. The article was more of a journaling exercise after reaching a point of frustration with living in my own discomfort zone. Perhaps you have had those feelings. You may be experiencing them now in some area of your life. I would love to tell you that after making that commitment to have enough fruit for today, I skipped happily down the road to success and fulfillment, never to be plagued by doubt, unbelief, and stagnation again. I am afraid that for me, it took discovering my purpose and coming to grips with who God really has called me to be. I realize that the fruit I desire resides within me. All God wants me to do is BE those fruits. I don't have to grow them or pick them- just be them.

God has called us to BE His children, and somehow, we have become driven by doing things that we think will help us DO. But before we can do anything, we must renew our commitment to be who God is calling us to be. We have to renew our commitment to begin this road trip and leave our discomfort zone. When we are committed totally to traveling the path that the Lord has for us, then we can do effectively the things that we need to live the life we deserve.

A Lamp for Your Feet
Make the decision to renew your commitment to leave your discomfort zone.

A Light for Your Pathway
Create in me a clean heart, O God, and renew a right, persevering, and steadfast spirit within me
(Psalms 51:10 AMP).

Lighting the Way......

How do you know that you are ready to make the commitment to travel?

Record your thoughts here:

CHAPTER TWO
PAUSE, PLUCK, AND PLANT

Making the decision to take a trip is often easier than deciding where to go and how to get there. Your decision will likely be influenced by other people and their travel experience. But this trip is different. Your decisions must be made based on your purpose and God's will for your life. That means that you will have to approach your journey differently. There are many paths and destinations to choose. This is an opportunity for confusion to creep in and delay your progress.

When we are faced with decisions and challenges or find our progress stalled, it is important to prune our thoughts and cut away things that may hamper our progress. Most of the failures that I have experienced have not occurred in the execution of the tasks, projects, or goals. Failure occurred while I was in the shower, driving in the car, and listening to others. Failure occurred when I chose to believe the facts that I could see versus the truth that I know.

In coaching, we call the voice that you hear (usually your own) in the back of your mind "the saboteur." The saboteur says things like, "Why are you doing this? You are too old, too fat, too poor, too uneducated, etc." The goal of the saboteur is to reverse your decision to travel. In a secular setting, it's nice to use a word like saboteur, and it is politically correct. But let's be very clear: the saboteur is the enemy, and he uses your voice and doubts to swindle you out of your destiny. I am talking about God's enemy, the one who comes to steal, kill, and destroy (John 10:10). If he can kill your destiny while it is still in your mind, then he thinks that he can abort your travel plans. That is why the mind must be renewed.

The mind is the garden of our dreams and aspirations. When productive, the mind provides fertile ground for your success. When unproductive, the mind creates a stony bed of failure, condemnation, and thoughts of inadequacy. Addressing this complexity, Paul encourages transformation by the continuous renewing of the mind (Romans 12:2).

My first gardening experience helped me understand the mind renewal process. In preparation, I researched plants and tools for the project. I also established a budget to set boundaries for my project. To reach our destination, we must research the Word of God so that we know where to plant our gifts and to establish His boundaries for our lives.

But even meticulous planning didn't prepare me for the weeds that would grow in the garden. I had to check each plant, identify any weeds, and extract them by the root. Our minds need weeding, too. We are instructed to pull down strongholds, cast down imaginations, and bring every thought captive to the obedience of Christ (2 Corinthians 10:4-5). That means we are to examine every thought as we think it and bring captive (arrest and detain) any thought that is inconsistent with the Word and will of God.

Initially, I was deceived by the weeds. Some weeds looked like flowers, at first. These plants had interesting leaves that I thought eventually would flower. But the weeds outgrew my flowers; only then did I realize that they were weeds. The same is true of our thoughts. We allow the deception of fear, doubt, and unbelief to grow alongside our destiny. We water these next to our dreams because we are accustomed to their presence. These weeds are more difficult to extract. If I had pulled them up when they were very small, they would have come out effortlessly. But allowed to grow, they were thick, tough, and stubborn. I was able to pull some of them myself, but my husband had to pull the rest. Some spiritual transformation can be done on your own with the help of the Holy Spirit through meditating on the Word. But there are times when you must get the support of other saints. Renewing our minds requires us to think and act differently. We must employ a "pause, pluck, and plant" strategy:

Pause

When my mind is racing and I feel anxiety approaching, I pause and say (often aloud), "That's not my thought!" That pause allows me to regroup and make a wiser choice about how to proceed. Opportunities to pause include the moments: before responding to confrontation, when you begin to doubt your ability, or when you have been distracted from your commitment to this road trip. This pause will also allow you to prioritize your thinking. Even good thoughts of work, children, recreation, and new relationships can become weeds if they distract you from the will of God.

Pluck

If the thought isn't true, honest, just, pure, lovely, of good report, virtuous, or praiseworthy, it must be plucked (Philippians 4:8). Allowed to grow, unproductive thoughts (yours and the expressed thoughts of others) will overcrowd your mind and toss out the Word, your dream, and your destiny. Arrest those thoughts and pluck them out before they contaminate your peace of mind. This may require you physically to remove yourself from a situation or avoid people and places that trigger unproductive thinking.

Plant

Unlike computers, we cannot delete files from our hard drives. Our complex mind allows us to store and replay memories, experiences, and thoughts. So like garden weeds, an unproductive thought can resurface. Therefore, we must plant something in its place- The Word and Godly fellowship. When we plant the Word about a situation, we reduce the amount of room available for unproductive thoughts. The Word is the ultimate weed killer, and it will deter future mind weeds. Godly fellowship with other like-minded believers will also help you grow.

Renewing and transforming are ongoing daily processes, not one time events. Thinking with a renewed mind determines our ability to live God's purpose, hear His voice, and keep our eyes on the road. Transformation is necessary to ensure that we reach our destination. Continue to pause, pluck, and plant - keeping your mind free of things that will delay your travel.

A Lamp for Your Feet
Unproductive thoughts are road blocks to the life you deserve.

A Light for Your Pathway
Do not be conformed to this world (this age), [fashioned after and adapted to its external, superficial customs], but be transformed (changed) by the [entire] renewal of your mind [by its new ideals and its new attitude], so that you may prove [for yourselves] what is the good and acceptable and perfect will of God, even the thing which is good and acceptable and perfect [in His sight for you]
(Romans 12:2 AMP).

Lighting the Way……

What thoughts have hampered your travel?

Record your thoughts here:

CHAPTER THREE
STOP PRETENDING

If asked to list ten endearing qualities about our best friend, we could rattle them off effortlessly. It is so easy to see the brilliance in the lives of others. However, if asked to list ten endearing things about ourselves, most of us would be hard pressed to come up with three or four. And the ones that we were able to muster probably would be connected to the things that we do: parenting, work, hobbies, etc. However, who are you, really?

When clients hire a life coach, they do so because they are ready to make changes in their lives. These changes can include changes in their behavior, moving to the next level in their lives, or simply gaining clarity and focus. The assumption is made that these changes require something outside of themselves. For example, "If I can just learn what to do, I can lose the 30 pounds that I have been trying to lose for five years," or "If I had…, I would be happier and reach my goals." And because I have done this so many times myself, I know that this method works, but it is short lived. I quickly revert back to the behavior that keeps me stuck in a place I don't want to be. It is a vicious cycle of excitement, apathy, and discouragement. There is an excitement to take on a new challenge. This is followed by apathy as a result of slow or no progress, and concluded with discouragement and feelings of failure resulting in a return to the discomfort zone.

Because we are so convinced that doing is the way to get past our limitations, we perpetuate this cycle. Even in the areas where we achieve some level of success, there is still limited fulfillment. That *doing* manifests itself in our everyday habits: working excessively, praying less, keeping up with the Joneses, overeating, etc. We try to make changes to the things that others easily can see about us. That's a natural response because if we lose weight, for example, we quickly get feedback on our progress. In return, society rewards us with its positive affirmation. But making the real changes, those that are the core to success, requires much more from us. It requires us to look at who God says we are versus the person that we have pretended to be to protect ourselves from the uncertainty of God's will.

Who God says we are and the character that we portray are often very different in many areas of our lives. This is an observation and not a criticism. Here's what I mean: God describes His people as fearfully and wonderfully made, people of power and authority, individuals with the ability to face adversity with certain victory, people of great wealth, and on and on. Is this the way that you are living today? In some areas, perhaps you are, but I mean fully and completely. So how do we experience the life we desire? Your immediate response probably starts like this, "I should do.... I should have..... I must change....." All of those things require you to do something, but I am requesting that you make a shift in your thinking. I am asking you not to consider what you must **do** to experience success in your life, but who you must **BE** in order to experience and enjoy success. Please notice that I said *be* and not become. Become implies that you are not that person already. I argue very strongly that you are that person NOW. It is that part of you that longs for more and has brought you to this book and your personal road trip.

It is important to acknowledge that you are who you need to be to live the life that God called you to live- Right Now! Before you lose the weight, get the degree, find a mate, get the promotion, you are that person. That is why you can set a goal and begin working towards that goal with fervor and determination. However, because your focus is on the doing and not the being, you perpetuate the cycle that I described earlier. Here's what happens. The real you does not allow you to become complacent and satisfied with the status quo. The real you is what causes your discomfort with certain areas of your life, so you give in to that and make a commitment to make some changes. You start out like gang busters with a new attitude and patterns of behavior. Then something strange happens: you become aware of your movement out of your discomfort zone, and the *protective you (the you, you have been pretending to be)* arrests the real you and locks it away.

Let me make some distinctions between the *real you* and the *protective you*. The real you is very clear about your inheritance as a child of the King. The real you has great ideas and can see the victorious end of a thing in adverse situations. The real you is often described as the authentic you - who you really were created to be. The real you holds your passions and is responsible for the goodness and wholeness that come out of you. The real you is fearless, which is why you can start so many things.

The protective you does just that. Its goal is to protect you from the world and, unfortunately, from the real you. The protective you forces you to pretend to be fearful, slothful, unfaithful, or whatever your issue happens to be. The job of the protective you is to keep the real you tucked away. The protective you will acknowledge your gifts, ability, and skills and still say, "Yeah but....."

So imagine that there are, literally, two completely different people living inside your body. Let me help you.

Imagine that you and your mother lived in the same body. There would be some similarity and familiarity, yet there would be constant conflict because you are both uniquely different. There would be times of great companionship and peace and other times of anguish, struggle, and unrest. When I talk about the real you and the protective you, I am talking about YOU. Both entities reside in you. There is always a conflict between who we were created to be and who we pretend to be. So the real you wants to make a change, and the protective you gives in to fear, doubt, and discouragement and aborts your travel.

I hope that you now at least understand the conflict that lives within you and that understanding brings some level of peace that will renew and refresh you. Paul illustrates this spiritual conflict when he talks about wanting to do good, but evil is always present (Romans 7:21). It was important for me to help you make the distinction between doing and being. It was important to identify and label the struggle between the real you and the protective you.

Having made that distinction, I believe the real you is ready to move forward. I believe that you are quite familiar with the you that you have been pretending to be. So we will spend more time in the next chapter getting reacquainted with the *real* you.

A Lamp for Your Feet
Stop pretending and give in to the *real* you.

A Light for Your Pathway
I will praise thee; for I am fearfully and wonderfully made:
marvelous are thy works; and that
my soul knowth right well
(Psalms 139: 14).

Lighting the Way......

Is the real you different from the person you portray daily?

Record your thoughts here:

CHAPTER FOUR
TAKE A FRESH LOOK

So, who are you? When asked this question, we automatically refer to the roles that we play. "I am a wife, a mother, an author, a speaker..." But my question is who *are* you, *really*? The question is not who have you become as a result of your life experiences, circumstances, and environment, but who *are* you, *really*? You may have to think back to who you were before the rejection, before the grief, before you learned to fear, or before you reached great success. Here are some more questions that might help you get there: What did you love to do before someone told you that it was dumb or unproductive (I am talking about moral, legal righteous things)? How did you feel when you were doing that? How are you feeling now as you ponder that? What you are getting, at this very moment, is a glimpse of the *real* you.

I immediately think of Adam and Eve. They walked around the garden naked and unashamed (Genesis 2:25). But they made some conscious choices in their lives, and the result was they became aware of their nakedness and immediately became ashamed. So I ask you, when did you realize that you were naked? Your nakedness is your vulnerability, your passions, and dreams. And the challenging thing is that the life that you deserve is tied directly to what you choose to do with your nakedness. For a long time, I made the conscious decision to cover my nakedness. I did this by suppressing my feelings and operating at about 70% capacity- okay 50%. I suppressed my feelings because I thought that it would protect me from being hurt. I suppressed my emotions because society has us convinced that emotions are not acceptable in the church, on the job, and in most relationships. We have been conditioned to be cool, calm, and collected.

I was recently facing a significant challenge in my life that would impact my finances and my career. I needed to be a part of several meetings to bring this matter to closure. My greatest concern was that I didn't want to cry in front of this group of men. With so much on the line, I should have been concerned with the implications of the decisions that were to be made. But I was concerned about controlling my emotions: I could clearly see the real me. I am VERY caring. I am full of compassion and love, and yes, I have lots of emotions, and they manifest themselves in tears. Joy, pain, fear, and love will produce my tears. That's who I am. And it is less of a burden to live that than it is to spend the rest of my life trying to change that. The tough, take-charge business person that I pretend to be has protected me from being hurt, but it has also led me to operate in denial of who I really am.

I have operated at 50% because I have gotten away with it for so long. Is the fact that I have been able to achieve some significant level of success in my life with only a 50% effort something that I feel good about? If God had only wanted me to use 50%, He would have given me only that much potential. So operating at this level keeps me clothed and makes me feel less vulnerable to risk, rejection, and failure.

I really want you to identify your own nakedness. It may require that you spend some time shedding the garments that you have spent years collecting and coordinating so carefully. Here is my request: Select a challenge that you are facing right now - relationship, career, habits, emotions, etc. Recall a time when the thing that you are struggling with was perfect. Focus on your surroundings during that time and take in the scenery. Now focus completely on how you feel in that moment. Do not focus on the things that you have and are able to do, but what you feel about yourself in that moment. That feeling reveals who you are, and it is not dependent upon anything that you do.

One of the first things that I challenge my coaching clients to do is to find their promise in the Word. I need them to be convinced that they can have what they desire to achieve in the coaching process, not because I am such a great coach, but because God has said that it is available to them. This takes the pressure off of the client. If God has said that you can have these things, then He will make the provision. But He needs you to be the vessel that He created you to be - the real you.

Here is my challenge to you: Before you move to the next chapter, I need you to reclaim who you are. You will do this by finding yourself in the scriptures. Who does God say that you are? What does He say that you can have?

I thought that I would save you some time and identify the excuses that you may come up with that will justify you declining my challenge:

1. I am a Bible scholar, and I am certain that I already know what the Word says about it. Unless you can recite the entire bible from memory, *meet the challenge.*
2. I will need to get a new study Bible or concordance. DON'T buy a thing! That is part of the deception - that you don't already possess what you need to be successful. It also delays you getting naked, thinking that you have to go out and purchase something, etc. Use what you have and *meet the challenge.*

3. I really don't know my way around the Bible that well. This is a good time to start, and *meet the challenge.*
4. I don't have time. You aren't worth the time that it will cost? *Meet the challenge.*

A Lamp for Your Feet
Take a fresh look at the *real* you.

A Light for Your Pathway
But his delight and desire are in the law of the Lord, and on His law (the precepts, the instructions, the teachings of God) he habitually meditates (ponders and studies) by day and by night.¹And he shall be like a tree firmly planted [and tended] by the streams of water, ready to bring forth its fruit in its season; its leaf also shall not fade or wither; and everything he does shall prosper [and come to maturity]
(Psalms 1:2-3 AMP).

Lighting the Way……

Who does the Word say that you are?

Record your thoughts here:

CHAPTER FIVE
GRAB YOUR TRAVEL GUIDE

I hope that you have spent some time getting reacquainted with who you really are and feel renewed and encouraged. Let's take this renewal a step further. An exploration of who you really are will reveal some facts about your life. Your experiences and life circumstances can present a challenge to your success. My role as coach is to help my clients gain clarity about their goals, fulfillment, process, and purpose. But that clarity can be obstructed by the facts that we see. Those facts can be from the past or present. So as we move forward, it is important to be clear about the facts that are seen versus the "truths" that we know. This distinction will fortify our commitment to renewal. Here are a few examples:

Fact: First quarter sales are down 40%.

Truth: The righteous work of your hand will prosper. You are a tree planted by the river. You will produce fruit in your season (Psalms 1:3). This is an opportunity to re-evaluate your plan and strategy for the year. Don't waste time second guessing whether or not you should have started the business or the project. Use this time to prepare for the opportunities that are ahead. Meditate on that truth and use the wisdom available to you to identify and maximize new opportunities.

Fact: Your marriage is in crisis.

Truth: Your breast does satisfy your husband (Proverbs 5:19). Or, you are a man of wisdom and integrity. In all that you experience in life, you can return each day to the bosom of your beloved. That is your refuge, sanctuary, and place of ministry. Whether the crisis is about money, employment, children, or infidelity, the marriage relationship should be the safe place for both the husband and wife. The crisis that you are experiencing is temporary, but the covenant of marriage is permanent. So avoid making permanent decisions to resolve temporary circumstances. Marriage is a ministry. When focused on that truth, you can endure and overcome that crisis.

Fact:You are in financial trouble.

Truth: *God will supply all of your needs according to His riches in glory in Christ Jesus (Philippians 4:19).* Your needs are not a surprise to God. He is well aware of your contribution to this situation, and yet He forgives you and entrusts you with His treasury. Walk in the truth of that forgiveness. All provision is from God's hand. Eating from the hand of a stranger opens the door for lack. The hand of a stranger includes looking to your employer, business, and relatives as your provider.

Fact:You don't know what your purpose is in life.

Truth: God called you and predestined you to live your life of purpose *on* purpose (Romans 8:29-31 AMP). It is so easy to see how great other people are yet ignore the greatness that God has placed in us. We take our gifts, abilities, and interests for granted and often fail to connect them to our purpose and destiny. You have something to offer the world. Find out what it is and trust that God will use it for His glory.

Fact: You need to lose 30 pounds.

Truth: God does good work, and you are fearfully and wonderfully made (Psalms 139:14). Without losing one pound, you are that! Embrace that truth. Come to peace with and accept it. Losing the weight will enhance who you are, not define who you are. Change your perspective and notice the impact it will have on your progress.

Fact: You are really overwhelmed with all your roles and responsibilities.

Truth: I agree with the song writer that "you are every woman (or man) and it's all in you." The Holy Spirit lives in you, so you can do all things through Christ who gives you strength (Philippians 4:13). If you are looking for strength outside of Christ, you will feel overwhelmed. You are anointed uniquely to do all that you are called to do. Take this time to discern what you are called to do versus what you *call yourself doing*. If it's a God assignment, then He is responsible for providing the resources of time, energy, and creativity.

Your issue may not be covered here, but I think that you get the point. Find the truth about your situation in the Word and meditate on that. Take some time to assess where you are and get re-energized by the truth. The facts are obvious, but the truth is the tool that will light the way and change your perspective. This shift in perspective will generate ideas and strategies to keep you on the road to the life you deserve.

Preparing your mind for success is even more important than getting an education or developing new skills. That is why I have devoted two chapters to ensure that we reinforce a sure foundation upon which our success will be built. In order to ensure that we are prepared to reach our destination, we must grab our traveler's guide. A traveler's guide tells you the things to do and what to expect when you reach your destination. The guide also gives you helpful hints that will make your travel more pleasurable. Our travel guide, of course, is the Word of God.

In addition to referring my clients to the Word about a situation that they are facing, I encourage them to establish a structure to remind them of God's promise of victory. A structure is something visible or tangible that will remind you of your commitment to renewal and the life you deserve. For example, several years ago, God began to reveal my purpose to me. This was a process that took several years, so there was plenty of time for me to get discouraged along the way. Ezekiel 1:8 describes the glory of God as *like amber.* If you think of a flame, the brightest part has an orange glow, like amber. That was so significant to me. I knew instantly that my purpose is to manifest the brightness of God's glory here on earth. At that moment, I didn't know how. I just knew that it was to be. That brought me great comfort - to at least know my specific purpose. Since then I have established amber jewelry as my structure to encourage me and keep me focused. It has sustained me while God has continued to grow me and prepare me to live the life that I deserve. Today, I know that I am to light the way through speaking, writing, and coaching. I am to be a vessel of the light, a container of the light, and I am to hold that light and light the way for those that I serve to reach their destiny.

A Lamp for Your Feet
The Word of God is the traveler's guide of truths.

A Light for Your Pathway
Sanctify them through thy truth: thy word is truth
(John 17:17.)

Lighting the Way……

What structure will you create to remind you of the truth?

Record your thoughts here:

SECTION TWO
REFOCUSING

I hope that you are encouraged, renewed, and re-energized. Our next step in preparation for our road trip is to get refocused. The emphasis will be on getting refocused in our relationships. To refocus means to change emphasis or direction (Webster Merriam Online Dictionary, 2005-2006). Relationships are critical to our being. But sometimes, in pursuit of our goals, we neglect the very relationships that are necessary to live the life we deserve. We will look at changing our emphasis and direction in Section Two.

CHAPTER SIX
MAKE EYE CONTACT

I was on my own with the children this particular morning. My husband was out of town, so I was in charge of the morning rush. The children know the morning routine very well. They also know that they can not turn on the television unless they ask first. And all of their morning chores must be completed before asking.

I had completed a few tasks the night before to help with the morning routine, so I knew that their backpacks were packed, the reading assignment had been completed, and all of the homework was signed and packed in its proper place. I proceeded to get myself ready for the day. It wasn't long before I heard my daughter calling me from the den, asking if she could turn on the television. My first concern was that she asked if her *brother* could watch television. I questioned her motives because even at two, my son was very capable of asking to watch his favorite television program on his own. She continued shouting her request up the stairs. I continued to get dressed, ignoring the ruckus that now included my son's billowing as well. They completed their morning overture with, "Mommie, Mommy! Mommmmmiiiieee!" as if I had gone deaf.

Finally, I could hear my daughter, who was six years old at the time, coming up the stairs. She said, "Mommy, we have been calling you. *We* (finally the real motive) wanted to know if we could watch television." I responded, "Sure, you could have watched television, but I was waiting for you to come and ask, not shout at me from the bottom of the stairs. As a result, you have wasted ten minutes that you could have spent watching your show. And now I am ready to go."

As I drove everyone to their designated place for the day, I couldn't help but think of my motives when I approach God. I pray and ask for things, telling God how I will use them to serve, or give, or benefit His work. But some of those things are for my own personal, spiritual, and financial benefit as well, and that's okay. God created all things richly to enjoy (I Timothy 6:17). So there is no need to sugar coat the desires of our hearts when we pray to make them seem super spiritual. As long as the desire lines up with God's Word and His will for us, our motives remain acceptable. But we are not tricking God when we try to conceal the root of our supplication.

We already could be enjoying the thing we seek if we would come into God's presence and seek Him face to face. I am certain that our road trip will be more effective and pleasurable if we make eye contact with the Father. Instead, we are more content to remain in the presence of the thing that we want and focus our time and attention on it instead. If my children had left the room with the television to come and have a face to face with me, I would have granted their request immediately. They had met the requirements for morning television. There are days when I respond to their long distance cries. I have shouted my permission from the other room on many occasions. But this particular day, I wanted to see their little faces, the faces that look like mine, and look into their eyes. I wanted them to know that my silence wasn't a "no" answer. It meant for them to come see me – face to face.

God so desires to see our faces lifted to Him. And in our eyes, He desires to see Himself. We have already met the requirement of salvation. Stop shouting at the Lord from a distance. Don't delay, or His response may be, "You could have had it all along and now it is too late. I have moved on." God's silence isn't a "no" answer. It is an invitation. Sometimes, we get so focused on achieving a particular goal that we let all of the other things in our lives suffer. A lot of times it is our relationship with the Lord. I encourage you to get refocused and leave the presence of the thing you seek, clarify your motive, enter His presence, and ask God for the things that you desire face to face.

A Lamp for Your Feet
When you find yourself stalled on the side of the road, get refocused and make eye contact with the Father.

A Light for Your Pathway
Seek ye the LORD while he may be found, call ye upon him while he is near: Let the wicked forsake his way, and the unrighteous man his thoughts: and let him return unto the LORD, and he will have mercy upon him; and to our God, for he will abundantly pardon
(Isaiah 55:6-7).

Lighting the Way......

What has drawn your focus away from your relationship with God?

Record your thoughts here:

CHAPTER SEVEN
INVITE HIM IN

My husband and I were having a discussion about the division of labor in our home. A very intense discussion! I presented my case like a prosecuting attorney. "I feel like I am always under pressure to keep things in order, meet everybody's needs, resolve problems, and fix everything. I'm always hurrying to complete the multitude of tasks on my list, and sometimes I look around and you are just standing there watching me run around like a chicken with my head cut off. You may even follow me from room to room just to watch me- What's with that?" My husband replied calmly, "I am waiting for you to invite me in." "What?" I said, "You see me struggling, and you are waiting for me to invite you in?"

After I regained my composure, his response made a lot of sense to me. Past experience has probably taught him not to interrupt my flow. I may be struggling with what I am doing, but there is certainly some method, rhythm, or zone that I am in at the time, and interrupting will only irritate me. So he stands there wanting to help, and hoping that I will tell him how to help. But I can't recall a time when I "invited him in." I usually ignore his presence (because I can't believe that he is just standing there!), and he eventually goes away.

Then I am left to complete the task alone and pout about how overwhelmed I am with all of my responsibilities.

As we wrapped up our discussion, my husband asked, "In the future, can you tell me how to incorporate my help into the things that you need to get done? Tell me the parts of the task that you want me to complete." Wow, that was easy! Then I began to think, "Who else is standing there watching me take on the world all by myself?" I began to imagine the Holy Spirit standing there, following me from room to room and place to place wondering, *When is she going to invite me in? When will she invite me in to help her be the best wife and mother that I know she is capable of being? When will she invite me into the small areas of her life that will empower her to handle the big things? When will she invite me in to address the fears and doubts in her heart? When will she invite me in to be her partner here on earth until the Lord returns? I promise that I won't interrupt her flow unless she is operating outside of God's flow. I certainly can't make a bigger mess of things than she makes on her own. God sent me here to help, and sometimes she just leaves me standing there as she struggles with the work that the Lord has set before her. What's with that?*

I really believe that God watches us struggle along living the *super hero* lie, trying to solve every problem, stretch the money, keep the house clean, deal with the problems at work, facilitate a peaceful home environment, etc. We read God's directives in His Word, and we set out on the path of good intentions to fulfill his Word. But we must acknowledge that there is no command in God's Word that we can keep on our own. We need the help of the Holy Spirit. We pursue love, peace, direction, obedience, and holiness in vain without the aid of the Holy Spirit. Our prayer time, meditation time, and study time are like unseasoned food without the presence of the Holy Spirit. It is the power of the Holy Spirit that allows us to walk and not faint.

When we ignore the important people in our lives, we make them feel useless and unnecessary. We perpetuate the lie that they are associated with a super hero. Satan is the father of lies, and we rebuke him in the name of Jesus. We need our spouses and loved ones to help on this road trip. We also need the guidance, direction, and empowerment of the Holy Spirit to maintain our souls. Both our loved ones and the Holy Spirit are vital to our lives, and they will not force themselves on us. Is the Holy Spirit outside patiently watching you struggling to live the life that you deserve? Invite Him in! Ask Him to stay!

You can not achieve this success alone. This success isn't just about you. In fact, it isn't about you at all. God wants others to be blessed by your victory - not just your victory upon completion, but your victory along the way. I encourage you to identify a Success Team. This team of people will hold you accountable in love. Invite them in, too!

A Lamp for Your Feet
Get refocused by creating a Success Team, and allow the Holy Spirit to be the captain.

A Light for Your Pathway
For the promise [of the Holy Spirit] is to and for you and your children, and to and for all that are far away, [even] to and for as many as the Lord our God invites and bids to come to Himself (Acts 2:39 AMP).

Lighting the Way……

Who are the members of your Success Team?

Record your thoughts here:

CHAPTER EIGHT
DON'T FORGET TO REMEMBER

We have talked about some important intimate relationships with God, the Holy Spirit, spouses, and children. But there are so many people who touch our lives. While our time is already divided and limited, we must honor and protect the relationships that support and allow us to be who God has created us to be.

One night about nine years ago, I was having trouble sleeping. I was restless and unsettled. I was weepy, and I couldn't stop crying. All I could think about was my father. Initially, I thought this weepiness was due to homesickness. Recently, I had moved away from home for the first time. My family was in Indiana, and my husband and I had just moved to upstate New York (837 miles away to be exact!).

I continued to lie there, weeping. My husband woke up and asked what was wrong. All I could say was that I was thinking about Daddy and I could not stop crying. He encouraged me to get up and write down all of the things that I was feeling in hopes that I would feel better. I got out of bed at 2:00 A.M. and began to write my dad a letter. I told him that I was thinking about him. I shared that I was afraid that I had forgotten to tell him thank you for some of the things that I appreciated most. Had I forgotten to thank him for all of the childhood vacations? I couldn't remember if I had thanked him for the simple things, like bringing home shrimp or White Castles ™ on Friday nights. Had I remembered to thank him for working double shifts and overtime to pay for my college education? What about my wedding? I couldn't remember if I had thanked him for welcoming my husband into our family. Had I thanked him for honoring my husband and respecting his home? Had I forgotten to thank him for graciously relinquishing his position as the number one man in my life to my husband, while remaining one of my best friends?

The uncertainty of remembering and the fear of having forgotten moved me to tears. As I completed my letter of gratitude and fond memories, I still couldn't rest. It was now 3:00 A.M., and I just wanted to hear his voice. I took a chance, and I called him. Surprisingly, he was awake (at least that's what he said). We talked for about an hour, and I told him that I had written him a letter and would mail it that day. I had remembered! With a sigh of relief, I finally fell asleep.

I had remembered to tell my dad how much I loved and appreciated him. I didn't take it for granted that he knew. I was given an opportunity to pour out my heart to him and let him know the impact that he had on my life. And he let me. His tough guy exterior couldn't hide the pride that he felt. In fact, he called me after he received the letter in the mail to, in his own macho way, say thanks and share that he loved and missed me, too.

That was in September 1997. In June 1998, my father died very suddenly at the age of 52. I found the letter among his personal things, tucked neatly in his appointment book. I was so glad that I hadn't forgotten to remember! Coming home to bury my father was one of the most difficult things that I have ever had to do. But I was overwhelmed by the peace and joy that I had. Despite the loss, I had the gift of knowing that nothing was left unspoken. While my father knew how much I loved him, I was given an opportunity to pour out my gratitude to him and to God.

All success is achieved in some relationship with others. Be sure to nurture positive, life affirming relationships along the way. The journey we face will be challenging enough, so be careful not to isolate yourself from healthy relationships. If God gives you an opportunity to remember today, pick up the phone, write a note, or send an email, but don't forget to remember!

Lamp for Your Feet
Get refocused by sharing the depth of your love with others. And allow them to share their love with you.

Light for Your Pathway
If one falls down, his friend can help him up. But pity the man who falls and has no one to help him up. Also, if two lie down together, they will keep warm. But how can one keep warm alone? Though one may be overpowered, two can defend themselves. A cord of three strands is not quickly broken (Ecclesiastes 4:10-12 NIV).

Lighting the Way......

With whom will you refocus and reconnect?

Record your thoughts here:

CHAPTER NINE
TAKE EXTREME MEASURES

We have done a lot of work to determine who we really are in Christ. We are getting refocused on our relationships. However, there is a relationship that we also need to sever. As we prepare for this road trip to the life that we deserve, there is an unwanted traveler packed and ready for the ride. There is no way to leave him behind without a fight, and it will be a fight to the death. So we must plan a murder. Yes, a murder!

It is time to murder the flesh. *For if ye live after the flesh, ye shall die: but if ye through the Spirit do mortify the deeds of the body, ye shall live* (Romans 8:13). Mortify means to deny or set limits. We should be *[habitually] putting to death (making extinct, deadening) the [evil] deeds prompted by the body…* (Romans 8:13 AMP). We have to make a conscious decision daily to murder the desires and deeds of the flesh. I have taken this a step further. I propose that my flesh and yours need to be murdered. Murder is the crime of unlawfully killing a human being, especially with malice aforethought (Webster's II New Riverside Dictionary Revised Edition,

1995). The two key components of murder are that this action is unlawful and done with malice and forethought.

Murdering the flesh is considered unlawful in the world that we live in today. Society encourages us to live without limits and to succumb to the desires of the flesh. The world acts as if we owe the flesh the pleasure that it desires. But we know that *we are not debtors to the flesh, we do not have to live after the flesh* (Romans 8: 12). We do not owe the flesh anything, and we are not obligated to serve the flesh. The flesh is to become subject to the spirit of God that dwells in us.

Whenever you try to exercise control over the flesh publicly, you are questioned, harassed, and even persecuted. When you abstain from going places and indulging in the flesh, you may be questioned or harassed about your decision. To those without Christ, exercising control over the flesh is unnatural and unlawful.

Murder also has some element of forethought. The murderer makes a conscious decision and establishes provision to commit the act. Premeditated murder is different from other degrees of murder because the murderer has given great consideration and established a plan to eliminate the victim. So we need a plan to commit the premeditated murder of the flesh:

Identify the Victim

We must ask the Lord to reveal to us the weaknesses and vulnerabilities of our flesh. Most of us already know them well. They are the things that sabotage and delay the success that God has planned for our lives. So we start by identifying the victim. Don't feel bad about the use of the word victim. Save your pity. This is no innocent victim. The flesh has committed many crimes against you and has caused you to violate God's Word or will in some way. It must die! But the Holy Spirit will guide you and give you insight into the area of focus for this road trip.

Study the Victim's Patterns

Our flesh often has a pattern. For example, I am prone to gluttony when I am tired and stressed out. Many Christians think that lust is solely a sexual issue. So they assume that they have addressed the lusts of the flesh because they are married, or they have their sexual desires under control. But lust includes anything that has the potential to take God's supreme place in our lives. Lusts of the flesh are things that violate and defile our temple. Anything that delays or interrupts our ability to be holy and acceptable and pleasing to God is born out of lust. So if God has given you instruction to do something challenging and you refuse, you have succumbed to the lust of the flesh. Our flesh wants to remain in our discomfort zone. God instructed you to do something else, and if you disregard His instruction, you have given in to the lust of the flesh through your disobedience.

I used the example of gluttony, which is a battle that I fight daily. It would not be so difficult if when I am stressed and tired I devoured an entire bowl of fruit or pot of steamed vegetables. No, my flesh craves something with grease topped off with a box of donuts, or some type of chocolate candy washed down with a soda. During these times, my flesh lusts after high calorie, low (no) nutrition foods. Overindulgence in these foods defiles my temple. The frequency and quantity of the foods that I consume leave me irritable and ill-equipped to handle physically the daily responsibilities God has entrusted to me.

I have studied the victim. I know the pattern. So I can develop a plan to murder my flesh in this area. I know that I usually can stay on track with a healthy diet during the day, but at night, I begin to crave the junk food. I know the pattern, so I can put things into place to break that pattern.

Find a Motive

When someone commits a premeditated murder, there almost always is a motive. Often that motive is greed or revenge. We also need a motive for the murder of our flesh. Our motive is our desire to please God and to uphold the values and principles of His Word. We want to murder the lusts of our flesh because they are in violation of those principles.

Find a Co-conspirator

There are often people in our lives who watch us struggle daily with the sins that so easily beset us. They sometimes feel helpless as they watch, observing that we had not made a conscious decision to mortify our flesh. These same individuals can now become your accomplice to murder the flesh. These individuals may be members for your Success Team. Perhaps you may need to establish a new Success Team for this issue. This person or group of people will help you with your plan and hold you accountable for your follow through.

Choose your weapons

Now that we know what we are up against, we have identified any behavioral patterns, and we have a support system in place, we must choose our weapons. We know that *the weapons of our warfare are not carnal, but mighty through God to the pulling down of strong holds (II Corinthians 10:4).* Therefore, we must use the weapons of the spirit given by God to overtake the stronghold of the flesh. When David prepared to fight Goliath, he chose a sling shot and five smooth stones from the brook (I Samuel 17:40). As we prepare to slay the giants and challenges that stand between us and the life we deserve, I propose that we select five smooth stones as well:

The Word

We have already used the Word to establish our motive for destroying the flesh. Our desire is to live a holy life free from sin and the lusts of the flesh. When you are confronted with a challenge that threatens your success, you rarely have time to grab the Word and begin to see what God has to say about the matter. That is why we started with the Word, so that when adversity comes we are already well equipped. So draw on that Word immediately when your challenges arise.

Meditation

After you have found encouragement in the Word, meditate on that Word. Memorize the scripture that encourages you the most. Select the scripture that will be your battle cry and repeat it to yourself over and over during the course of the day. Bury it in your heart.

Faithfulness

Take stock of what you really believe to be true. Challenge yourself to believe God's Word. Demonstrate it by your obedience and faithfulness to be free from sin and to press on. Be persistent and consistent one day, one hour, and one minute at a time. Remember, this is not an over night stay - this is a long journey. Do not get weary in well doing; don't faint (Galatians 6:9).

Fasting/Prayer

There are many books and articles written about fasting. In addition to discussing the spiritual benefits of fasting, they also describe fasts that were practiced in the Bible. These books may be helpful to review and provide insight into your area of concern. I believe that fasting is an essential weapon to use in combating the flesh.

Giving

Giving is a powerful weapon for overcoming any stronghold in your life. Whenever I am experiencing a significant challenge, in addition to finding scripture, meditating, and fasting, I also sow a seed into the kingdom as a memorial. I know that God honors that seed.

Your personal arsenal may include more than the five smooth stones I have listed. Whatever they are, keep them close and accessible. You will recall that David gathered five stones, but he only used one to slay the giant. For our purposes, I believe that the one stone that will slay the giant in our lives will be faith and faithfulness. We need all five stones, but we must have the unwavering faith that God's Word is true and that He will bring us to a place of victory every time. Without faith, we are just carrying a bag of rocks.

Face the Giant

All of our planning is just a conspiracy to commit murder until we actually confront and kill the flesh. This confrontation, simply, is putting the plan into action. Whatever you have gleaned from the Word and are prompted by the Holy Spirit to do, implement those things. Getting started may be difficult, and maintaining will be even harder. Continue to stay in contact with your co-conspirators/prayer partners and keep meditating on God's Word. Throw your stone of faithfulness at the uncircumcised Philistine in your life, and he will surely fall. The Bible doesn't record Goliath's last words, but be warned the flesh is a smooth talker. When you begin to execute the plan to murder your flesh, it will plead for mercy and try to negotiate. Don't listen! You have come this far, so do the deal and kill the flesh.

Remain Vigilant

Once you have committed the murder, you must remain vigilant. Sin is often a manifestation of another issue in our lives. Unfortunately, sin is not like literal human flesh. When you murder a human in the natural, that person ceases to exist. He will not show up at school in a week or so; he is gone forever. But our flesh is more like a zombie. You can kill it, but left unchecked, it may resurrect itself and come out looking and smelling worse than it did before (dead things stink). That is why it is necessary to go through the process of killing it everyday, even if you think that it is dead. That is why you have the other four stones. Through study, prayer and fasting, meditation, sowing, and faithfulness, we keep the flesh in the grave.

A Lamp for Your Feet
Do not negotiate with the lust of the flesh that stand between you and the life you deserve.

Light for Your Path Way
And if the Spirit of Him Who raised up Jesus from the dead dwells in you, [then] He Who raised up Christ Jesus from the dead will also restore to life your mortal (short-lived, perishable) bodies through His Spirit Who dwells in you.
So then, brethren, we are debtors, but not to the flesh [we are not obligated to our carnal nature], to live [a life ruled by the standards set up by the dictates] of the flesh. For if you live according to [the dictates of] the flesh, you will surely die. But if through the power of the [Holy] Spirit you are [habitually] putting to death (making extinct, deadening) the [evil] deeds prompted by the body, you shall [really and genuinely] live forever
(Romans 8:11-13 AMP).

Lighting the Way......

What extreme measures do you need to take today?

Record your thoughts here:

CHAPTER TEN
DESIGN YOUR ROAD MAP

Now that the flesh has been murdered, we are free to design our life diagram and road map. Developing a plan is not only a prudent business move, but a biblical mandate: *And the Lord answered me and said, write the vision, and make it plain upon tables, that he may run that readeth it. For the vision is yet for an appointed time, but at the end it shall speak, and not lie: though it tarry, wait for it; because it will surely come, it will not tarry (Habakkuk 2:2-3).* We have asked God to reveal His will and His purpose for our lives so that we can live our purpose and reach our destiny. The Word tells us that the next steps are ours. We must take that revelation and write it down. We do that to memorialize God's instruction and to use it as the foundation to determine how we use our God given resources. From this, we draft a plan that describes where we are going. This plan must take into account where we are now and the steps that we need to complete in order to take us where we want to go.

This plan becomes our road map on our journey to the life that we deserve. Using His purpose as our guide, the

Holy Spirit will direct us on this journey of purpose. Without this road map and the guidance of the Holy Spirit, we wander around life aimlessly. But when we spend time in God's presence, we are able to discern the path that we should take. Establish a plan that identifies your goals and objectives. What are the short term and long term goals? What will you need to get there - family support, financial means, education, certification, etc.? Establish a timeline and bench marks to evaluate your progress. You may also want to include incentives to reward your progress.

As life coach, I must interject that there must be some level of resonance and excitement for you about this road trip. You may not be excited about the stops that you will need to make on the way. But you certainly should be excited and energized about the destination. If you are not excited about where you are going and the end result, your planning will be ineffective and futile. Allow the *real* you to design the road map and not the *protective* you that is full of fear and unbelief.

Also, consider carefully the impact that your chosen path will have on other areas of your life, health, relationships, finances, etc. Remember that our destination is the life we deserve. These things are all included in that life. Don't allow these things to hinder or discourage you, but be aware of them so that you can make informed decisions. When you hit difficult times or you become exhausted, reviewing a well thought out plan will allow you to refocus and remember why you started the journey in the first place.

Follow the Map

I find this part the most challenging in my own personal experience. My gifting and education in administration allow me to craft a feasible and effective plan. However, sticking to the plan is my biggest challenge. Knowing what to do does not ensure success. Knowing what to do and doing it persistently and consistently will be the only sure path to the life we deserve.

Once you have established a God ordained road map, stick with it. Execute the plan! Yes there will be minor set backs and obstacles, but keep moving forward until the Holy Spirit tells you differently. Establish incentives for yourself if they will help you follow the map. For example, when I finish this writing project, my husband will buy me a new perfume. Set yourself up for small victories on the journey so that you can be faithful to finish.

Be Open to Detours

Another struggle that I have is remaining flexible and taking detours. Once I have overcome the challenge of sticking with it, I find it difficult to switch gears. But even with the best thought out plans, obstacles and opportunities will come. It is important to allow your plan to be a road map for your feet and not a noose around your neck. You may have planned to take this journey as a direct flight on a jet plane. But God may be calling you to travel by bus with many stops and different traveling companions. For example, I am a highway driver. I would much rather stay stalled in traffic than to take side streets through town. But I have wasted a lot of time sitting on the highway waiting for things to clear up. Being open to detours may allow you to move faster and give you an opportunity to see things that you may have missed on your planned route.

In addition, it is important to be flexible so that we can be sure that we are going in the right direction. I don't mean that we are second guessing God. I am saying that we must always be sure that we got it right. Are our motives still pure? Assess if your initial route was based in fear. Have you now moved into faith?

Lamp for Your Feet
Your road map will be specific to you and your gifts,
calling, and purpose.

A Light for Your Pathway
The steps of a [good] man are directed and established
by the Lord when He delights in his way [and He busies
Himself with his every step]
Psalms 37:23 (AMP).

Lighting the Way……

How will you begin to design you road map?

Record your thoughts here:

SECTION THREE
RECOVERING

Even after restoring and renewing the freshness and refocusing by changing direction, there will still be road blocks. Given that, it is important to consider how you will recover from setbacks. To recover means to get back, make up for, and to find identity (Webster Merriam Online Dictionary, 2005-2006). In this section, we will discuss how to recover from obstacles and setbacks on the road trip to the life you deserve.

CHAPTER ELEVEN
REMEMBER YOUR FIRST LOVE

We know that it is in God that we live and move and have our being (Acts 17:28). We realize that God is the very air we breathe. But along the way, we begin to take this ability to breathe for granted. Many asthma sufferers have to get breathing treatments during certain weather conditions. When the air is humid and the ozone ratio is high, they have difficultly breathing. On other days, their asthma may not bother them at all. Breathing comes naturally, and they may even skip the preventive measures that ensure better breathing during adverse weather conditions. Many asthma suffers are prescribed an inhaler, and like most medications, patients initially use them faithfully. But over time, the users become confident and comfortable that they have their condition under control. They may even misplace the inhaler. But when an asthma attack comes, they are left vulnerable and scrambling to find their medication for relief.

The same can be said of our relationship with the Father. When we start our journey, it is like breathing fresh air for the first time. We like to sit close to God and inhale His freshness because we need to hear from Him to get direction. But as we get comfortable and confident in our faith, we venture further and further from the throne of God. I don't mean that we journey into sin, but our focus is on any number of other things. As we discussed in Section Two, we lose our focus. We take the fresh air for granted. It is easy to grow close to God when we need answers. We draw near when we need a word about our purpose, ministry, family, career, spouse, health, etc. But once we have that answer, we are off and running to operate in our new revelation. God provides the inhaler of prayer and praise to usher in His presence daily. But sometimes, in our pursuit of good works, we misplace it and are left scrabbling when adversity comes. We are searching for God. He has remained on the throne, but we have wandered into the fog.

It is so easy to become consumed with the cares of this world. These cares even include the things that God has blessed us with, like our families, jobs, and ministries. But we must remember to return to our first love. It is important to fill our lungs with the freshness of God's presence daily. Maintaining God's place and presence in our lives is the preventive medicine that we need to foster gratitude in our hearts, both when we abase and abound.

Returning to our first love means seeking the *presence* of God and not the *presents* of God. We will always have needs and desires, and God wants to fulfill every one of them. God wants us to live the life we deserve more than we do. But the most important time spent with God is just loving on Him in prayer, praise, and worship. I am reminded, here, of my natural father. My dad's greatest joy was to surprise us with gifts. He especially liked to surprise me with things that he heard me mention that I would like to have. But in all of that, some of the best times that I remember with him were the times that we just hung out together. I would go for a ride in the car with my dad, with the windows down and music playing. We may not say a word the whole time. However, when we returned home, I remember thinking what a great time we had together, just being in each other's presence. I didn't expect any gifts. I didn't ask him for anything. I just wanted to be with him.

God has placed great visions, dreams, and purpose inside of us. Our major purpose is to be God's ambassador here on earth. In doing so, our purpose may bring us into great positions of responsibility, notoriety, and influence. Regardless of the role we play in God's plan, we must be careful, even in our service, to remember the One we serve. When you encounter delays in your travels, the quickest way to get on the road again is to return to your first love.

A Lamp for Your Feet
Seek the face of your first love, not the gifts of His hand.

A Light for Your Pathway
You have persevered and have endured hardships for my name, and have not grown weary. Yet I hold this against you: You have forsaken your first love. Remember the height from which you have fallen! Repent and do the things you did at first. If you do not repent, I will come to you and remove your lamp stand from its place (Revelation 2:3-5 NIV).

Lighting the Way......

Is there anything in your life that is causing you to neglect your first love?

Record your thoughts here:

CHAPTER TWELVE
DON'T DESPISE HUMBLE BEGINNINGS

O nce the thrill and the excitement of beginning this road trip have waned and the reality of the challenge that lies ahead settles in, we find ourselves feeling inadequate, unprepared, and overwhelmed. After the excitement of living in the newness of God's light subsides, we are able to see how far we have left to go. At this point, it is easy to give up and become discouraged relative to the progress that we are able to make. Even though the closer to the end we get, the more difficult things often become, we must remember that God has already completed the story, and He sees a victorious life ahead.

Once we have reached the victory of one goal, God will give us the vision for the next one, and we find ourselves at the beginning once again. The beginning is difficult, especially on the heels of a significant victory or promotion in another area. But do not despise humble beginnings. Rest assured that the end of the thing will be greater than the beginning. *The end of a matter is better than its beginning, and patience is better than pride (Ecclesiastes 7:8 NIV).* This scripture is an awesome reminder of our motive and heart condition.

When we feel overwhelmed and disappointed about our progress, pride is often at its root. At some point, we have compared ourselves to others who seem to be moving effortlessly faster and more successfully than we have. This pride can lead to frustration, depression, discouragement, and may open the door for failure. We will never cross the state line on our road trip if we do not continue to journey along the path that God has for us. Our goal is to get there.

I ran my first half marathon a couple of years ago. Well, I *finished* my first half marathon; I had to walk a lot of it. My goal was simply to get to the end and to finish the race, not finish first, but to finish. While I ran, there were senior citizens that flew past me. (Yes, I know they were senior citizens. I looked up their bib numbers and stats in the newspaper the next day!) While I was struggling at mile eight, they were cordial and chatting as they sailed past me. I noticed that whenever I began to reflect on how many people were passing me and how easy the race was for them, I began to slow down. I became discouraged, and I wanted to quit. However, when I focused on my race and the goal of completion, I remained focused to the end. I reminded myself of how far I had come already and that I only had five miles to go. I also had to consider my own unique circumstances. I was a novice runner and was nursing an injury to my ankle. When I considered those things, I was able to recover from my discouragement and keep going.

One asset I enjoyed during the race was a close friend that trained and ran with me. My injury slowed me down quite a bit. But my friend ran at my pace even though she could have run faster. As long as I was willing to continue the race and not give up, she was willing to run beside me. However, if I had given up, I am certain that she would have continued without me. I would have had to ride the bus to the finish line alone in defeat.

Humble beginnings are a great opportunity for monumental success. Knowing that we are renewed and refocused gives us the push we need to recover or get back on the road.

A Lamp for Your Feet
A humble beginning is the perfect platform for extraordinary success.

A Light for Your Pathway
The glory of this latter house shall be greater than of the former, saith the LORD of hosts: and in this place will I give peace, saith the LORD of hosts
(Haggai 2:9 NIV).

Lighting the Way......

What are the benefits of your humble beginning?

Record your thoughts here:

CHAPTER THIRTEEN
FAN THE FLAME

Distraction and discouragement will not only come at the beginning of your road trip, but they may be a challenge at any point. Identifying your God given purpose is a liberating experience. Many get comfortable with simply knowing their purpose. Others seem paralyzed by the uncertainty of what to do next. While identifying purpose is important, the victory rests in living that purpose with persistence and consistency. Paul admonishes Timothy to *stir up (rekindle the embers of, fan the flame of, and keep burning) the [gracious] gift of God, [the inner fire] ... (2 Timothy 1:6 AMP)*. Our passion for purpose is a gift to us. We, too, must fan the flames of our gifting, calling, and anointing every step of our journey.

When rekindled, the flames of a fire become hotter and more intense. When a campfire dies down, it doesn't provide much light and warmth. But when the embers are stirred, the campfire provides a comforting heat. Those around the fire may need to remove their hats or jackets to remain comfortable around the fire. That same campfire provides direction to other campers. They can smell the fire and see the flickering flames in the distance guiding them to the campsite.

God has given us purpose, dreams, passions, talents, and ministries to glorify Him whether we recognize or exercise them. Fanning the flames means putting what we know to do into practice. As you fan the flames, others will be drawn to you like a campfire. They will see God's glory and feel His warmth through you. Perhaps they may remove their fleshly garments because of your intense fire. They will shed habits and ungodly thinking as the spirit of the Lord burns brighter in you. Burdens will be lifted. Bodies will be healed. Souls will be saved.

"That sounds great," you say. "I want to be on fire for God!!!" Well, you need something to burn. Let's start with any new bad habits that we have picked up on this road trip. Also include unrenewed thoughts and a lack of focus. That's enough to get a fire going. Then use prayer, fasting, and the Word of God as the accelerant. And allow the Holy Spirit to strike the match and ignite your spirit. Now that's a fire! This fire costs something. The expense to you is keeping the flesh murdered or burned up. Your spirit man must emerge intact from the flames.

It is time for us to burn in the place that we have been called for such a time as this. How diligently and consistently we fan the flames will determine whether we are a feeble flicker or a roaring fire for God. We must keep the flame roaring because someone else's destiny depends on it.

When you lose intensity and effectiveness, recover by fanning the flame. Here are few fanning techniques:

1. Remember to use your Success Team. They will fan your flame.
2. Have you completed the last God given task? Act on the directives of the Holy Spirit **immediately**. Follow through on witty ideas and God given inventions. This way you are careful not to grieve the Holy Spirit and limit your intensity.

3. Beware of firefighters. Firefighters are people and circumstances used by Satan to hose you down with deception, distraction, and discouragement.
4. Keep the symbols of the vision and purpose before you. Touch your purpose everyday. Refer to the structure that you created earlier to help you focus.

A Lamp for Your Feet
Fan the flame to recover from distraction and discouragement.

A Light for Your Path
I have been reminded of your sincere faith, which first lived in your grandmother Lois and in your mother Eunice and, I am persuaded, now lives in you also. For this reason I remind you to fan into flame the gift of God, which is in you through the laying on of my hands. For God did not give us a spirit of timidity, but a spirit of power, of love and of self-discipline (2 Timothy 1:5-7 NIV).

Lighting the Way......

What can you do today to fan the flame?

Record your thoughts here:

CHAPTER FOURTEEN
USE YOUR WEAPONS

In preparation for our road trip, we have discussed the weapons that we need to conquer the giants and other enemies standing between us and the life we deserve. Like Goliath, these enemies operated from a distance. So we were able to plan and execute our fight from a distance. However, as we move forward in purpose, the closer we get to our success, the more intense the enemy will become. He will realize that this long distance fighting is not working, and he will begin to move in tighter and closer. You must be prepared to recover with hand to hand combat.

Like most young girls, I was taught that fighting is not lady like. I was advised to use other methods to resolve conflict, like negotiating, talking to an adult, or walking away. In the fifth grade, there was a young girl who announced that she did not like me. I didn't know her at all, so I couldn't rationalize what I had done to make her dislike me. She informed me and the entire class that she wanted to fight me. I discussed this with my mother and told her that I was afraid because I didn't think this could be resolved without me getting attacked.

My mother, in her ultra lady like manner, advised me to avoid the girl or talk to the principal. However, following the usual parental advice, I was shocked at her next directive. She took me into the bathroom and stood me in front of the mirror. She began to point to all of the vulnerable areas of the body. She told me, "Focus on the throat. When you see an opening, hit her in the center of her throat. That will knock the wind out of her and startle her. Then just keep on hitting her until a teacher or adult comes." I couldn't believe that my mother was teaching me how to fight in the bathroom. She also added that I wouldn't get into trouble with her and my dad for defending myself. I was still afraid, but not unprepared. I did have to use my mother's counsel and "fight school training." The fight wasn't a TKO victory for me, but it wasn't a beat down either.

That was the first and last time that I was involved in a fist fight. But as you get closer to your destiny, you will experience more intense warfare. Our *adversary roams around like a lion seeing whom he may devour* (I Peter 5:8). It is a constant battle. However, we are not unprepared. There is our God. Our assurance is that *He shall cover thee with His feathers, and under His wings shalt thou trust: His truth shall be thy shield and buckler* (Psalms 91:4). In addition, *He layeth up sound wisdom for the righteous: He is a buckler to them that walk uprightly* (Proverbs 2:7). Like my mother, God gives us assurance that we can defend ourselves from the enemy, and He exhorts and instructs us through His Word on how to do so. God says that HE IS our shield and buckler. That means that He is a shield that protects us and defends us from the enemy and his schemes.

But a buckler is an interesting and diverse weapon. It is a small metal hand shield used for close combat. A broad shield defends long range or distant attacks. The buckler is described as a deflector, a blinder, and a metal fist (Wikipedia, the free encyclopedia, 2006). When used as protection, the buckler deflects the thrusts of an attacker. However, it also has a different purpose. The user can conceal his weapon behind himself and, using the element of surprise, strike his opponent. The use I have become most acquainted with is the metal fist. The old French definition of buckler is "metal fist." When the blades of opponents were locked in combat, the buckler (metal fist) could be used to punch the opponent in the face.

I am glad that the Lord is my shield, but Halleluiah for the buckler!!! My shield is good for the areas where I have experienced victory. The enemy can keep firing darts, but they will not hit me. However, there are other areas where Satan knows he must get close in order to provoke or fight me. I am usually in hand to hand combat with him over my finances, my children, balancing my time, and being productive. Because our buckler is the truth of the Lord, and the truth is His Word, we must stay prayed up and studied up. Otherwise, we are defenseless.

When we are new in Christ, we rely on the milk of the Word as our shield. However, as we grow in the Word, we learn to eat the meat of the Word and use our buckler. Satan knows that he must come close to us if he has any chance of drawing us off the path. We must be so strong in the Word of the Father that we are able to punch Satan in the face. And when we have him surprised and startled, we must keep on punching him with the metal fist of the Word until Holy Spirit releases us.

Satan will provoke you, so there is no penalty for defending yourself from the enemy. In fact, God expects us to initiate attacks on the very face of the enemy. That is why he gave us weapons. We must be faithful to show up for battle daily with clean, sturdy, and dependable weapons. When we go for days without studying and meditating on the Word, we show up for battle with unreliable, outdated, and faulty weaponry. This will limit your ability to recover from challenges and detours. In the meantime, you will have been distracted and strayed from the path to the life you deserve.

So remember to come dressed for battle daily and use your weapons.

A Lamp for Your Feet
The closer you get to your destiny, the more personal the enemy's attacks will become. Recover by having your buckler ready.

A Light for Your Pathway
He layeth up sound wisdom for the righteous: he is a buckler to them that walk uprightly
(Proverbs 2:7).

Lighting the Way......

In what areas of your life do you need a buckler?

Record your thoughts here:

CHAPTER FIFTEEN
BE GOOD TO YOURSELF!

One of the definitions for *recover* is to identify again (Webster Merriam Online Dictionary, 2005-2006). Earlier in this book, we spent a considerable amount of time talking about the *real* you and who you really are. Sometimes, along the way, we can become so consumed with the journey that we lose sight of who we are. It becomes necessary for us to recover or to identify who we are again.

When I was a teenager, my mother bought me a jewelry box with the inscription, "Be Good to Yourself, Mom." For years, I have quoted her advice. It took me a while to learn the true wisdom of her words. Sure, I did things necessary to keep myself from hurt and harm. But she said to be good to myself, not protect myself.

She was talking about more than scheduling a spa appointment and eating directly from the ice cream carton. She meant that I should fulfill the dreams of my youthful heart, do things that would bring me true happiness, and dare to live the life I deserve. She didn't mean for me just to do the things that allow me to remain in my discomfort zone. God's grace allows us to realize the dreams of a youthful heart and live the life we deserve. That grace is available even when our dream seems hopelessly deferred. As we physically mature, maintaining a youthful heart is critical to being good to ourselves and reaching our destination.

Many adults are intolerant of youth and teenagers. These youth are the epitome of potential and energy. Most often, they have not succumbed to the pressures of life and have not allowed those pressures to steal their joy. But there is no need to be envious of a teen's carefree attitude. It is possible to rekindle that inner joy and peace by releasing some of the adult baggage that we carry. We must guard our hearts against nonessential things that try to creep into the suitcases of our lives. That's a step towards being good to yourself.

I dated a guy for a long time because I thought it was the "right" thing to do. After ending the relationship, I had an overwhelming peace and joy. He was a nice guy, but not the *right* guy. This difficult decision was the first conscious stop on my road trip to being good to myself. As a result, I took a European vacation, became serious about graduate school, and learned to enjoy my own company!

We are on a wonderful journey to possess God's best for us. We are responsible for carrying our own luggage on this trip. We need to begin to sift through our dreams, our goals, and passions, packing only things that will help us on our journey. It may not have been pleasurable, but if it was character building and helps you move to the next port of call in life - pack it! But if it is anger, bitterness, insecurity, jealously, laziness- trash it! After all, we will be carrying this luggage ourselves. We also must discern the difference between things that are good *to* us and things that are good *for* us (relationships, habits, jobs, etc.).

I think that my mother wanted me to make decisions for myself based on who I am and my destiny. She wanted me not to be selfish, but to create a self that is worth sharing. When your bags get heavy on this trip, be good to yourself by taking a moment to sort and repack. This repacking will allow you to recover and identify who you are and what you really need. So I share the wisdom of this sage with you: "Be Good to Yourself! Sincerely, Raquel."

Lamp for Your Feet
Being good to yourself includes recovering your identity - who you *really* are.

Light for Your Pathway
THEREFORE THEN, since we are surrounded by so great a cloud of witnesses [who have borne testimony to the Truth], let us strip off and throw aside every encumbrance (unnecessary weight) and that sin which so readily (deftly and cleverly) clings to and entangles us, and let us run with patient endurance and steady and active persistence the appointed course of the race that is set before us, (Hebrews 12:1-3AMP)

Lighting the Way......

How can you be good to yourself today?

Record your thoughts here:

SECTION FOUR
READY

When you pack for a trip, you usually have the sense that you are forgetting something. Usually, you haven't forgotten anything at all. You just feel this sense of caution. Well, in the previous chapters, we have renewed, refocused, and learned ways to recover. And I believe we are ready to begin our road trip to the life we deserve. That will be the focus of this final section.

CHAPTER SIXTEEN
GRAB YOUR BAGS

A s we finish packing for this exciting road trip, maybe you are feeling that things will be decidedly different from now on. The preparation alone has required you to make a change. You probably anticipate that there are more changes to come if you are to reach your goal. By now, you also may have realized that the challenges that you will face are not the real issue. *You* are the issue. You don't need to be fixed because you are healthy and whole and of great value. You just have made some adjustments to your thinking and perspective that allow you to maximize and appreciate your value. I am encouraging you to sort through and carefully pack your thoughts, so you leave room for the real issues in your life.

Currently, you may not be comfortable with this new way of thinking and being. However, I am confident that you have addressed some things that may have been holding you back. You are now ready to tackle some of the challenges forcing you to change - right now. In order to address an issue, you must first determine what it means to you and what values are associated with it.

Why is living the life that you deserve important to you? Why do you deserve it, anyway? If your answer is that you need to make more money, or you want to fit into a pair of jeans that you wore in high school, or you are tired of not having a mate, I encourage you to ask yourself if that is a compelling enough reason to move to action. I suspect that if it were, you already would have experienced victory in this area or have a framework to retain that victory. I believe that you want victory in this area, but you haven't reached the root of your desire to change.

Your ability to live the life that you deserve hasn't become real to you. I believe that once you expose the root of the desire and identify the values associated with it, you can see quite clearly where you are. You may discover that what you have been focusing on isn't really important to you, or it may create such emotion that you are propelled into action. These emotions can be joy, anger, compassion, etc., but they become the root or the fire that burns within you. That fire will allow you to clarify and feel how important this really is to you.

Our entire time of preparation for this trip has been about change. We have had to change our minds, our relationships, and direction. And you know by now that these are the changes that will usher you into living the life that you deserve. But why is living the life you deserve so important to God? What does He say that you deserve? You have already found yourself in the Word. You have researched and studied scriptures about your desire that should help you answer this question. The changes that you desire to make in your life are somehow connected to your own values and the things that you find important, yet you continue to feel frozen at the doorway of destiny.

There are a few things that keep us from taking the first steps and making a change. The first is the fear of the unknown. We become anxious when we perceive there is information that we don't know about a situation: Will you get the bid? Will your organization file for bankruptcy? Will she leave you? But if you had those answers, what could you do about it? Very little! In those instances, your time is better spent addressing the areas that we have covered in this book, and others like it. You are ready to make a change.

You may have started our time together focused on the many things that you must do to make the changes in your life necessary to reach your destination. And yes, there may be many things for you to do. But what we have been focused on is changing your mind, your will, and your emotions - your soul. Our main tools in making these changes are the Word of God, the Holy Spirit, godly relationships, and the gifts that God has entrusted to us. We are a spirit being that has a soul and lives in a body. Our soul houses our mind, will, and emotions.

Taking the time to do this soul work allows us to step away from the cares of this world and sort things out. It allows us time to **renew, refocus, and recover**. When we do this, we clear the way to embrace change and see things from God's perspective. None of this has changed our circumstances, but it has changed our *attitude* toward the circumstances. This attitude adjustment will allow us to make prudent, wise, and productive decisions that will put us on the path to our goal.

I am sensing that you are ready. You're ready to breathe in all that God has for you through the nostrils of the *real* you. Breathe in all that He has for you as if for the first time. You have your road map and your traveler's guide, and you are ready to go. The way has been lit! Let's go!

A Lamp for Your Feet
Changing your perspective is more important and profitable than changing your circumstances.

Light for Your Pathway
For I know the plans I have for you, declares the LORD, plans to prosper you and not to harm you, plans to give you hope and a future. Then you will call upon me and

come and pray to me, and I will listen to you. You will seek me and find me when you seek me with all your heart (Jeremiah 29:11-13 NIV).

Lighting the Way......

Why is taking this road trip important to you?

Record your thoughts here:

CHAPTER SEVENTEEN
CROSS THE THRESHOLD

You have done a lot of work so far, and I believe you have reached not the end, but the beginning. You reach a threshold when you come to a point where you cease to be effective. Perhaps that's what brought you to this book. What you were doing before was not producing the results that you want. But you cross a threshold when you leave something behind and move into another realm. It's like leaving the shore and stepping into the Jordan River. Let's cross over!

Your question at this point may be, "What do I do now?" Your inclination is to ask someone else just to tell you what you should do. Should you start the business? Should you go back to school? Should you confront your children? Life would be so much easier if someone would just give you a Word from the Lord. If only God would just come, sit on the edge of your bed, hand you a "to do" list, and hand draw you a road map. It would be great if He would tell you the date and time of any future road blocks. Unfortunately, it doesn't happen this way. But you already have within you and around you what you need to live the life that you deserve.

We have focused on making changes that will result in us living the life we deserve. Here is the secret that you may have discovered already. When you are renewed, refocused, and have the ability to recover, you *are* living the life you deserve. We still need to make this road trip, but we don't have to wait until we get there. *There* is already in your heart. You can see it and feel the pleasure of it already. Knowing this, I believe that you are holding your next steps in your heart. They have been there all of the time. The essence of who you really are has known. However, your focus on the problems or challenges ahead has made you deaf to your own voice and that of the Holy Spirit.

To get to the answers that you seek, look at the things that you have been procrastinating about for the last six months. What has you afraid? What things bring you great joy that you don't take the time to enjoy? Look beyond the obvious - like needing a job so you can pay your bills. Instead, embrace the viewpoint that you need to take a job that will pay your bills and allow you to grow in your calling and purpose. It may not be THE job, but it will allow you to move towards it.

If you feel overwhelmed at this point, that's an indication that what you deserve is much bigger than you can even imagine. That's good because God doesn't expect you to do it alone. If He allowed you to reach your destiny and purpose on your own, you could take the credit and the glory. This would open the door for pride and rebellion. Since the Holy Spirit is the captain of your Success Team, He will lead you to people who will be like streams and feed the river that God wants to flow through you.

As we proceed to the threshold and doorway to take our journey, please be encouraged. Remember that God promised living waters would flow out of your belly (John 7:38). That is God's promise to you. When you remember to renew, refocus, and recover, God's river will water you. A river has a sense of organization. It flows in a particular direction and is fed by specific streams. But this organization does not make the river predictable. And your road trip will not be either.

There are times when the river is calm and even, and we like for God to flow this way. In the dry season, the river gets low, and there is concern about provision. The waters that flow through us are living waters. If we are experiencing a draught, it is unlikely that it is God's fault. It is likely that we have encountered a road hazard. Perhaps we have been dependent on a stream that has dried up. Or we have dammed up the streams that are supposed to feed us with sin, doubt, fear, unbelief, and inaction.

Perhaps the overwhelmed feeling you have is caused by your thoughts about how high the river is and how quickly the streams are feeding you. Things are moving and changing so quickly that it is difficult to get a handle on each issue and establish a plan to address it. If that is what you are feeling, I am inclined to say that this is a time of moving from *knowing* your purpose to *being* your purpose. It is a mandate to *live* your purpose. Yes, it is time for you to do something. It's time to get going.

Take a quick moment to review your road map. What's the very first step? This is a defining step - one that will launch you from fear to faith. Don't think big. Think purposeful! What can you do in the next 24 hours that will move you in the direction that God is leading you? It could be as simple as asking for what you want from someone with the authority to give it, writing out your purpose and vision statement, journaling what you are feeling, or hiring a trained professional, like a consultant, therapist, business coach, or life coach.

Whatever the action, it is yours to take and unique to your purpose and destiny. I am confident that you are ready. You have been preparing for this moment in time your whole life. Give in to it! Surrender to it! Make the Change! This is the end of our time together, but the beginning of a new day for you. It is a day with lots of work ahead, but unlimited possibilities. The result will be that you are living the life that you deserve. You've been dreaming about it. Now hit the road!

ABOUT THE AUTHOR

"Lighting the Way" is the mantra for Gary, Indiana, native, Raquel R. Robinson. Whether as an author, speaker, coach, administrator, or friend, Raquel believes her calling is to encourage others to live the life they deserve. With training as a co-active coach from the Coaches Training Institute, she works alongside her husband as the CEO and Success Coach of Making a Change LLC. Together, they light the way by providing executive coaching, life coaching, and consulting services to individuals and organizations. Raquel is the resident Life Coach for both *Keeping Family First* and *Inspired Living* magazines.

While enrolled as a freshman at Indiana University, Raquel continued her professional modeling career, based in Chicago, IL. The balancing act between school and career resulted in a Bachelor's degree in Organizational Communication and national ad placements in Elle, Essence, EM, and Vogue magazines. Robinson was Miss Gary in 1988 and placed third in the state competition for the Miss America Pageant. These experiences encouraged Raquel to provide inspirational workshops designed to facilitate the spiritual and emotional growth of girls and women.

Following her retirement from the runway, Robinson earned a Master's degree in Communication Studies at Purdue University and has fifteen years experience in both nonprofit and higher education administration. She also taught Communication courses as an adjunct faculty member at the State University of New York in Oneonta and Broome Community College (Binghamton, NY). Robinson currently is the executive director of a non profit organization in the Detroit metropolitan area.

She and her husband Henry have a seven year old daughter, Alexandria, and a three year old son, Michael. The Robinsons are members of Word of Faith International Christian Center in Southfield, Michigan.

To schedule an introductory coaching session, a speaking engagement, or to order additional books, write:

Raquel R. Robinson
Making a Change LLC
P. O. Box 787
Walled Lake, MI 48390-9998
Or
Email : Raquel@makingachangellc.com

Breinigsville, PA USA
14 March 2011
257638BV00001B/7/A